W9-BOF-900

A Song
Called Hope

ARTHUR GORDON

The C. R. Gibson Company,
Norwalk, Connecticut 06856

Text copyright © MCMLXXXV by Arthur Gordon
Published by The C.R. Gibson Company
Norwalk, Connecticut 06856
Printed in the United States of America
All rights reserved
ISBN 0-8378-5081-9

Introduction

‿

SOMEWHERE at this moment…
>   A baby takes his first step.
>   A five-year-old reads her first word.
>   A job-seeker sends out a resume.
>   A couple exchange marriage vows.
>   A housewife tries a new recipe.
>   A traveler boards an airplane.
>   A doctor prescribes a medicine.
>   An invalid takes it.
>   An agnostic enters a church.

What do these diverse members of the human race have in common?
Something elusive.
Something intangible, invisible.

Something enormously important.

Something called hope.

Think about it for a moment. Behind every action, beneath every endeavor lies this quiet, persistent, creative force, giving strength to all who believe in it, and call upon it, and blend it into their lives.

In this book I'd like to talk about hope and ponder it and perhaps learn more about it. And I begin (how else?) by hoping. Hoping that the words set down here may help someone, somewhere, to learn to practice hope, lean upon it, live more confidently because of it.

Everyone should try to make friends with hope. Because there's no better companion in the world.

Arthur Gordon

I

WHERE there's life, there's hope, the old saying goes.

True enough.

But the reverse is truer still: Where there's hope, there's life.

The wonderful thing about this life-support system is that it's always available. It's around us all the time, and we use it constantly, even when we're not aware that we're using it.

Consider:

In every week there are one hundred and sixty-eight hours. If you spend fifty of those hours sleeping, what are you doing with the rest?

You are hoping. Large hopes. Small hopes. All manner of hopes.

You're hoping it won't rain on the day of the picnic. You're hoping there will never be a nuclear war.

You're hoping your scratchy throat won't turn into a cold.

You're hoping that your old car will hold together for a few more shaky miles. That your child will get better grades at school. That you may get a raise or a tax refund. That love is stronger than hate. That no one will notice the run in your stocking—or the spot on your tie. That someday, somehow, you will manage to be a better person than you know you are.

If hope is the fuel we run on—and it is—why don't we pay a little more attention to it, think about it, try to understand it better.

We really should. Next to love it's the most important four-letter word in the world.

II

MORE than a century ago Emily Dickinson wrote these lines:

> *"Hope" is the thing with feathers—*
> *That perches in the soul—*
> *And sings the tune without the words—*
> *And never stops—at all—*

A small feathered creature singing in the bare branches of the human soul. A poetic image—so lovely that one is tempted to look no further.

But arrayed behind the image are deeper questions. How did that feathered creature get there? What enables it to sing so bravely? Why does it never stop?

How did it get there? Logic might answer:

"Somebody or something must have put it there." But behind this answer looms an even larger question: What was that Something? Who was that Somebody?

How does it manage to sing so bravely? All one can say is that this seems to be its nature. A spider spins. A sunflower turns toward the sun. And hope keeps singing its cheerful song because that is what it's designed to do. But again the fundamental question remains unanswered. If hope sings because it was designed to sing, who wrote the song?

Why does it never stop? This much is clear: It never stops because it is the needed force that lifted man from darkness and obscurity and keeps on lifting him despite all the failures and setbacks, all the heartaches and discouragements. Hope never stops because if it did everything else would stop.

Perhaps the Creator Himself needed hope in order to bring the universe into being and then have the patience to see it through.

Perhaps the hope we sense in Him is what we see reflected in us.

III

Hope is intimately tied to beginnings; of this I'm certain.

You're not going to start anything without hope of a successful conclusion.

Unless you hope strongly enough, intensely enough, you may never start at all.

In any endeavor, two thirds of the battle is won simply by taking the first step. All too often through the years I have let myself be held back by lack of confidence, fear of failure, sometimes just plain inertia or laziness.

But I've learned that if you force yourself to

make the first move, mighty forces will come to aid. The act of beginning starts the flow of power. But those who never begin never feel that power.

Between hope and action lies a chasm, deep but also narrow. It can be bridged by an act of will, a decision that says firmly, "Yes, I will take steps to make this hope a reality. And I will take the first step now."

Hope—the spark that ignites the actions that make the dream come true.

IV

Iᴛ's easy to think of hope as something fragile, a flame that flickers in the winds of adversity, constantly on the brink of being blown out.

But is it so fragile, really?

How can anything be fragile that has endured ever since man and woman first walked the face of the earth?

It was there long before recorded history, a dim but persistent spark in the mind of the first primitive person to tame fire or fashion a stone axe.

And it echoes in the earliest words that have filtered down to us through the centuries. Five thousand years ago in Egypt there was a man named Ptah-hotep, a sage whose teachings were revered by the people of his day. And what was at the heart of these teachings? A man, said Ptah-hotep, might achieve power and fame and fortune, but "it is the man's kindly acts that are remembered in the years after his life."

Where was the hope in that? It was in Ptah-hotep's patient belief that people were capable of accepting such a blue-print for living. Hope in the perfectability of people was alive in Egypt fifty centuries ago, and it's alive today.

❦

Even in places where it should be utterly crushed, trampled to death, hope still survives. If ever there was such a place, it was the infamous World War II concentration camp at Buchenwald, in Germany. I saw it myself a few days after it was liberated by General Patton's troops: the corpses stacked like cordwood, the gas chambers, the ovens, the gallows, the human skeletons, some living, some dead.

There were other camps as bad or worse.

And yet…

And yet survivors of such hell-holes reported over and over again that prisoners who some-how kept hope alive were the ones who remained alive themselves.

They hoped for an Allied victory.

They hoped for a chance to escape.

They hoped for a day of liberation.

They hoped for ultimate reunion with their loved ones, visualizing that day so strongly that hope somehow held at bay the horrors that surrounded them.

At Buchenwald a handful of prisoners who had been physicians formed themselves into a shadowy medical society. They read scientific papers to one another. They bribed the guards to obtain medicines. They fashioned crude surgical instruments. With the help of electricians and engineers among the other prisoners, they even managed to build a primitive X-ray machine.

Hope kept them going. Hope that they could dilute the ocean of pain that surrounded them. Hope that they could help their fellow sufferers. That's what brought them through.

Sometimes when the daily recital of rape and robbery, murder and mayhem in the daily press makes me wonder about the human race, I remember a story told by Mother Teresa of Calcutta, a grocer's daughter from Yugoslavia who goes around her adopted city in India helping people so poor, so degraded, so miserable that one wonders how the spark of life continues to flicker in them.

Yet Mother Teresa sees even in these unfortunates a trace of nobility. Mother Teresa calls it "the greatness of the poor." To make her meaning clear, she tells of the time she took some rice to a starving family someone had told her about. This family had not eaten in days. Mother Teresa could see the emaciation of the parents, the hunger in the hollow eyes of the children.

When she handed the rice to the mother, the woman divided it into two parts and started to leave the room.

"Where are you going?" Mother Teresa asked.

The woman said, "Next door they are hungry also."

The flame of hope in the world is kept alive by people like that woman.

No, hope is not a fragile thing.

V

THE Irish poet W. B. Yeats wrote four lines that seem to surface in my mind more and more often as the years glide by:

An aged man is but a paltry thing,
A tattered coat upon a stick... unless
Soul clap its hands and sing, and louder sing
For every tatter in its mortal dress.

What makes it possible for soul to clap its hands when troubles come and the fires of life burn low?

Two things, probably.
Gratitude for good days that lie behind.
And hope for good things still to come...
In this world or the next.

VI

HOW do you practice hope when you're feeling anything but hopeful?

Years ago I had a fishing companion who was older and wiser than I. He wasn't a psychiatrist, but he would have made a good one.

We were fishing in one of the tidal creeks that wind through the Georgia marshes where I live. I had managed to snag my hook in a hidden oyster-shell bank six feet below the surface. "Hopeless," I muttered, jerking furiously, my rod bent almost double. "I'll have to cut the line."

"It might not be hopeless," my friend said, "if you'd just relax for a couple of minutes. There are some friendly crabs down there. If you'll stop ranting and raving and give them a chance, one of 'em will try to eat the shrimp on your hook, and in the process he may free the line for you."

Sure enough, in five minutes a friendly crab dragged the line sideways and freed the hook.

Which led to some conversation about hope and how to increase your ability to maintain it.

"You have to remember," my old friend said, "that hope is a state of mind. So is hopelessness. If you can alter your thought patterns, you can move from one state to another.

"For instance, when you find yourself taking a negative view of something, as you did just now with your snagged hook, label it hopeless if you like. But then go one more step and add a phrase like 'And yet,' or 'But even so,' or 'Well, maybe...'

"No matter how bleak the prospect, in every case there has to be some hopeful possibility—in your case a friendly crab—that lies beyond the difficulty. Reach out to that. When you do, you'll find that your mind can't hold two opposing ideas at once. One always displaces the other.

"If you'll remember that," said my old friend, blowing the smoke from his pipe into the lazy Georgia afternoon, "you'll be able to inject hope into almost any situation."

Another remedy for hopelessness that I've figured out all by myself is to be open to the manifestations of hope that surround us all the time.

Hope is contagious.

If you let yourself come into contact with it, you're likely to catch it.

So watch for people who have it and demonstrate it:

The kid down the block who washes windows and mows lawns because he believes the money will help him to become a doctor some day.

The woman with a possibly terminal illness who smiles and quotes Browning: "The best is yet to be."

The girl who ran the New York marathon not long ago, all 26 miles of it, on crutches. She finally came in—last. But she finished the course.

If you can't find any such examples in your immediate surroundings, try reading the diary of Anne Frank, the young Jewish girl in Holland who lived and died under the Nazi terror and yet (and yet!) was able to write, "In spite of everything I still believe that people are good at heart."

Hope—it enfolds some people like a shining mist. Let some of it rub off on you.

VII

I'T'S easy to be hopeful when things are going well. It's when things are going badly that hopelessness comes around with its two dreary companions: the impulse to stop trying, the temptation to quit.

Sometimes it takes raw courage not to give in.

During the closing years of the last century there was a man in our family, who, through no fault of his own, went through some very trying times, so difficult and threatening—family legend says—that he thought seriously of leaving home and starting a new life in New Zealand or Australia or some such far off place.

I'm told that he sat up all one night trying to reach a decision. He was no poet, but in the dark

hours before dawn he wrote a few lines of verse—
you can hear nineteenth century echoes of Kip-
ling and the martial ring of Sir Walter Scott. The
verses were directed at himself. But perhaps they
have something to say to all of us:

The bugles sound retreat, the banners fall,
The hosts of eager allies melt away.
Many marched bravely with you. Of them all,
Few will stay.
Now fade the cherished hopes that once were bright
Now slowly sinks from sight the dying sun.
Is there an answer in the gathering night?
There is one.
Pick up that broken blade with weary hand.
Shout that this disappearing sun will rise.
Only the lost cause, the last stand,
Wins you the skies!

So he did fight on. I like to think that finally
when the sun rose and his banner streamed once
more in the wind, the word emblazoned on it
was Hope.

VIII

ONCE I made a special trip to Kansas to ask a man about hope. I remember that visit very well because no one, before or since, has impressed me quite so much as the man I went to see: Dr. Karl Menninger, dean of American psychiatrists.

We sat in Dr. Karl's office in the famed Menninger Foundation in Topeka. Outside a mild December wind stirred the evergreens. Inside, Navaho rugs covered floors and walls. Pre-Columbian Indian artifacts crowded cabinet shelves. Family photographs were on window-sills. Books were everywhere.

Wearing a big square turquoise ring, with turquoise cuff links in his yellow shirt, my host sat behind a desk overflowing with papers, pamphlets, paperweights, apples, and a three-gallon tin of popcorn ("Best way to buy it—you get three kinds—have some!"). Underneath the desk lurked Celeste, a brown poodle presence of infinite sagacity and rather unfortunate breath.

"Hope," said Dr. Karl reflectively, leaning back and peering at me owlishly through horn-rimmed glasses with eyes both discerning and kind. "It's a basic ingredient in human life, all right. Still, not much has been said or written about it. St. Paul knew how important it is; he put it right up there alongside faith and love. If you look in the *Encyclopaedia Britannica* today you'll find pages and pages about faith and columns about love. But hope—poor little hope—she's not mentioned at all!"

The ancient Greeks, Dr. Karl said, didn't think much of hope. They were fatalists. They believed that a person's destiny was fixed and inescapable, and hope a cruel illusion—"man's curse", Euripedes called it.

But St. Paul's Jewish heritage, with its age-old hope of a Messiah coming to rule over a better world, and his Christian belief in immortality made him a missionary of hope in an almost hopeless world. "It took a lot of courage," said Dr. Karl thoughtfully, "for Paul to stand up and tell those people that hope was real and that it was almost as important as faith or love."

He went on to talk about the importance of hope in teaching. "If you ever hear a teacher say a student is hopeless, you've got a hopeless teacher on your hands." And of its role in medicine. "I trust we're seeing the last of hopeless doctors telling patients that their case is hopeless. Once I saw a feeble-minded child recover. Medically, her case was hopeless, but she recovered anyway. So hope was there all the time; we just didn't see it."

Laboratory experiments, Dr. Karl said, seem to indicate that hope is the lifeline that often makes survival possible. Rats and other animals in stressful situations survive quite well so long as they can see or sense some possibility of escape. But once hope is removed, they give up and die very quickly.

"If you lose all hope," Dr. Karl said, "you stop trying. And you stop caring. That won't do. I think each of us is put here to help dilute the misery in the world. You have to believe that you can influence the larger problems of life by making small decisions of your own. You may not be able to make a big contribution, but you can make a little one, and you've got to try. That's a form of hoping too."

We went outside, finally, and walked through the gray twilight with Celeste ranging mercifully downwind. Dr. Karl's mind was richly furnished, so far-ranging, so alive that it was impossible to hold him to one topic. We talked of prison reform and the Navaho's sense of beauty and the future of space travel and the origins of chess.

And I remember thinking that, having come to Kansas to ask about hope, I was walking with the answer. This man was the embodiment of hope; his whole life was a reflection of it. All the books, all the teachings, all the insights were based on the assumption that the misery in the world can be diluted, that man can push back the frontiers of knowledge, that reason can prevail over prejudice and ignorance, that love is stronger than hate. The voice of Dr. Karl was the voice of hope.

Later, as I left the Foundation, I saw some words of the philosopher George Santayana mounted in large black letters on the wall:

We must welcome the future,
Remembering that soon it will be the past.
And we must respect the past,
Remembering that once it was all that was
humanly possible.

I like that last line.

It implies that what was once beyond our grasp is now conceivable, or even obtainable.

It's a line full of promise.

A life-line of hope.

IX

Henry THOREAU, the New England philosopher, once urged his readers to "print your hopes upon your mind."

Visualize them clearly, he meant.

Don't settle for vague yearnings or fuzzy dreams.

Summon up definite pictures of hopes being realized, of dreams coming true.

Hold these pictures in your conscious mind, clear, vivid, distinct, until they sink down into your unconscious mind.

Once your unconscious mind absorbs them, it will work ceaselessly, day and night, to transform the realizable wish into a tangible reality.

You won't even have to remind it.

It will remind you.

X

"ALL hope abandon, ye who enter here."

I used to think those grim words that Dante saw above the entrance to the Inferno were placed there to add further misery to sinners consigned to everlasting torment. Faced with the prospect of endless pain, they were being denied even the solace of hope.

But now, on further thought, I wonder if the purpose of the words might have been to protect hell itself, protect it against hope. Those who entered were told to leave hope behind because if even a spark began to glow, all the darkness of hell would not be able to put it out.

And hell could be hell no longer.

XI

ALL of us know times when the fires of hope seem to burn low. When they do, we go around expecting the worst to happen. We're afraid to attempt anything new or different because we're convinced that the chances of failure outweigh the chances of success and if nothing is going to work, if it's impossible to improve things, if the outlook is hopeless, why try?

What's the cure for this condition?

Time is one remedy. Wait a while. Hope is persistent. Sooner or later she will come back.

Meantime it might help to remember, when you wake up in the morning, that the world around you contains tremendous affirmations of hope:

Spring treading on winter's heels, with snowdrops and crocuses leading the way.

Summer, autumn, winter in unfailing pro-gression.

Dawn displacing darkness, rainbows following storms, tides that always come in again, comets that return on time to the split second. No matter what happens in small human lives, the great clock of the universe still ticks.

And on the day that's facing you, hope herself whispers that something may come along to re-kindle the flame: a new friend, a new experience, a new insight, even a new book may say, "Why are you treating hope like a stranger? Stop slam-ming the door in her face. Make friends with her! Invite her in!"

If you do, you can be sure of one thing.

She'll come right in.

The French novelist, Gustave Flaubert, once wrote: "The principal thing in the world is to keep the soul aloft."

What will do that?

Work won't do it, play won't do it, success won't do it, money won't do it.

Hope will do it.

Because hope gives the soul wings.

XII

I LOOKED up the word "hope" in my big dictionary this morning. "Hope," says Mr. Webster, is "desire accompanied with expectation of obtaining what is desired."

In other words, hope isn't merely wishing or wanting, hope is also expecting to receive, or achieve, or improve, or whatever. That little glow of expectation is what makes hope a more powerful attitude than merely wishing or wanting.

More and more doctors are becoming aware of this power. Medical science is finding that the attitude of the patient is just as important as the remedies or medicines administered—probably more important.

How does it work? Well, if you have a health

problem and you hope, strongly and confidently, to get well, you are constantly creating the mental image of a healthy self. It's almost as if the mind says to the body, "You may be sick at the moment; nevertheless I see you as recovered in the near future." And something in the body says, "Well, if this cheerful concept of me exists, I had better make an effort to live up to it, hadn't I?" Then it proceeds to do so.

"Hope deferred," says the Bible, "maketh the heart sick."

Yes, that's true; it does.

But hope applied—ah, that may make the heart well. And the rest of the body, too.

XIII

IN his famous *Essay on Man*, Alexander Pope wrote: "An honest man's the noblest work of God."

A century later Robert Ingersoll, the well-known atheist, sardonically reversed Pope's line: "An honest God's the noblest work of man."

Nevertheless, when his brother died, it was this same Robert Ingersoll who wrote, "But in the night of death, hope sees a star, and listening love can hear the rustle of a wing."

You can shut hope out for a little while, or even for a long while.

But in the end she usually has the last word.

XIV

"To be seventy years young," Oliver Wendell Holmes once remarked, "is often far more cheerful than to be forty years old."

Can growing older really be a hopeful thing?

Yes, if you can deal with a certain number of "ifs".

It can be hopeful if you believe that each age you pass through has its advantages as well as its limitations.

If you retain the capacity to welcome change, so that new ideas and new experiences do not dismay you.

If, as the years pass, you grow more skilled in your work.

If you manage to become more tolerant, more

generous, more understanding where other people are concerned.

If, gradually, you come to know who you are and have the courage to be it.

Two thousand years ago Cicero said that old age is "the crown of life, our play's last act."

A hopeful thought.

But you have to work to make it come true.

XV

RELIGION...the word means "bind together", doesn't it?

Bind what? The splintered fragments of human personality, perhaps. Bind with what? Two things, mainly: faith and hope.

"Why art thou cast down, O my soul," cries David in Psalm 42, "and why art thou disquieted within me?" Anyone who is discouraged must ask these questions. The Bible's answer follows instantly in the next four words: "Hope thou in God."

Hope that since He made you He understands you perfectly.

Hope that He is constantly aware of you.

Hope that He cares what happens to you.

Hope that He is love.

The Easter story of the Resurrection is the most stunning proclamation of hope ever heard on this planet. It aims squarely at our deepest fear: the fear of extinction, the fear of ceasing to be. Death, says the Easter message, is not the end. It's a new beginning.

"In my Father's house," said Jesus the night before His crucifixion, "are many mansions." What those mansions are like we do not know. Perhaps they are solar systems in other galaxies. Perhaps they are ascending stages of spiritual development. Whatever they may be, the assurance that they exist has given to countless millions the conviction that death is not an ominous finality, not a blank wall, but a door leading to realms of inconceivable brightness.

Faith and hope are the keys to that door.

Book design by Elizabeth Woll
Text set in Meridien